Beyond the Individual

Beyond the Individual

Expressions of the Greater Intelligence

Mark R. Unger

Copyright © 2017 Mark R. Unger

All rights reserved with the following single exception granted:

Limited, short excerpts from the content herein may be quoted freely in print or digital form, provided that credit is given to this book title and author and that care is taken to not place them in a different context. For more than a few excerpts or of a greater length permission must be obtained from the author.

ISBN-10: 0692976922
ISBN-13: 978-0692976920

Life is *thought*,

so think well and live well.

Table of Contents

Introduction	1
Terminology	5
1. The Experience of Illumination	9
2. The Greater Intelligence	23
3. Advice for the Seeker	53
4. Supplementary Topics	73
5. Some Words about Bucke	91
Ending Comments	95
Acknowledgements	97
About the Author	99

Introduction

As the term *self-consciousness* implies, it is centered on the individual—a realization of self-identity. We all have it so it is taken for granted. A consciousness higher than self, though, goes beyond the individual and is not so common. Has anyone not at some point wondered about the nature and meaning of life beyond its physicality? Questions along this line of thought have no universally accepted answers so there must be found a means to validate one's current beliefs or search beyond them, which is ultimately a personal quest for knowledge that can be appreciated only through the experience of expanded spiritual consciousness. Whether knowingly or not Illumination is the attainment that is sought, which permanently enhances the recipient's perspective of existence in a most profound manner, the source of which is the Intelligence that brought everything into existence. However one chooses to conceptualize or call that Intelligence at present, it is merely the starting point of a spiritual quest.

This work is intended to be a personal testament to the reality of Illumination (commonly called cosmic consciousness) and serve as a general guide to understand what it is and how it expands personal perspective. It is not a personal philosophy or derived from any study. Although the only real proof that Illumination is genuine is in having the experience for oneself, there is no specific method or procedure to guarantee an eventual illuminating experience. In other words, it is not like performing certain actions to obtain a known result, as though this were a demonstrable physical science project. The variables are the degree of determination and sincerity of oneself as well as one's current degree of personal inner development; attaining it is for the Self and mind together, not the mind alone. All paths to it are necessarily experiential and require more than an intellectual approach. All that a recipient of Illumination can do for others is to describe the path that he/she took (so to speak) and provide advice on the direction to go.

The purpose of reading descriptions of Illumination is not simply to have an idea of what it is like, but to assist in identifying it if and when it comes and prevent misidentifying lesser degrees of enlightenment. This difference might sound subtle, but it can affect one's outlook—striving to have a particular experience versus being open to whatever may come. Since I am describing what was learned through experience and am not trying to convince anyone of what to accept or believe I make little or no attempt to justify the content, wanting only to present food for thought. As such, this content is intentionally written concisely and must be read as a whole for the correct context.

While some parallels and similarities (besides some definite differences) can certainly be found between my writings and other authors, organizations and schools of thought, everything stated herein derives from my own experiences. Having lived within so-called western culture all my life, this is the backdrop of my frame of mind and the reader-audience that I write for. Although the experience and knowledge learned is profound and pronounced to the recipient, satisfactory description is beyond the limitations of linguistic expression; however, that is all that we have to convey detailed information to each other. Therefore, my choice of words, analogies and descriptions can represent only a best effort.

Terminology

Any attempt to describe an experience that is not so common will have difficulty with terminology. Terms used may come from a colloquial, religious, philosophical, metaphysical or scientific reference, depending on what the recipient of Illumination determines to be most descriptive and how he/she chooses to relate it to others. The following terms are defined for use within the context of this book and are not necessarily the same as used by others.

Belief system: Any religion or philosophy that has tenets, doctrines or reason and rationale to explain the meaning of and reason for life, which may or may not include an acknowledgement of a God, gods or some kind of guiding Intelligence.
Cosmic Consciousness: A term originated (or at least popularized) by Dr. Richard M. Bucke to signify the next stage of consciousness above self-consciousness, marked by a sudden and extremely brief drastic shift in awareness, but having a permanent effect. [I make a minor distinction by assigning a name to the experience itself (capitalized 'Illumination' as defined below)

because of its brevity, while its effects are what is lived with thereafter.]

Creator God: A generic term for any concept of an intelligence that is responsible for the forming of our physical universe and life.

Ego: Personal identity as one sees oneself; the source of vanity, self-importance, and self-esteem.

Enlightenment: Basically this refers to the acquisition of limited, specific knowledge, comprehension or insight into some issue from outside of oneself as though "out of the blue". Such knowledge comes to the mind without expanding consciousness.

Greater Intelligence: A name of sorts for distinguishing the aspect of intelligence of *Thought* (defined below) from It's manifestations. This term (shortened to G.I.) is of my own construct and is used simply to avoid connotations with existing religious and philosophical concepts and terms. This term is explained incrementally in chapter 2.

Illumination: Capitalized, it refers to a sudden and brief state of consciousness outside of physical and metaphysical reality that grants knowledge with comprehension regarding the nature of existence. Unlike enlightenment, this is an experience of one's very being.

Metaphysics: In a general sense and as used here, whatever is not physical or subject to what we call physical law, but still is associated with the physical universe.

Mysticism: Perspectives and practices of an inner nature that assist in striving for direct personal communication or communion with the Intelligence that is responsible for bringing the universe and life into existence.

One: Capitalized, this word was used by the philosopher Plotinus as a name for totality and is essentially equivalent to my use of the word *Thought*.

Recipient: The term that I use to refer to a person who has experienced (i.e., received) Illumination. [Although everything stated herein is my personal testament to the experience and what can be learned from it, there are some aspects that I intuit or surmise to be likely common to all and are partly corroborated by Dr. Richard Bucke in his book *Cosmic Consciousness*.]

Self: The spirit-identity of oneself.

Spirit: The animating force within every individual lifeform without distinctions being made; it does not cease to exist when the body dies. [I do not use the word *soul*, because that is often used to separate the human spirit from all other spirits.]

Spirit-identity: The accumulated life experiences from all incarnations that give an individual spirit a sense of identity (of being unique) to differentiate it from other spirits.

Thought: Capitalized and italicized *Thought* refers to the Intelligence that gave rise to the universe and permeates all that exists physically and non-physically as manifested expressions. Not to be thought of as a god in the usual sense—this is described in chapter 2.

Totality: Everything that pertains to the existence of the physical universe, with or without regard for the Greater Intelligence within. [Totality and *Thought* are almost interchangeable words.]

Universe: My use of this word is for the all-inclusive totality of the manifestation of *Thought*. If there are such things as theoretical multiverses they are within this total manifestation.

Regarding gender: Throughout this book, no distinction is intended between male and female as regards to Illumination. Simply to avoid combined terms such as *he/she, his/her*, etc., only one gender is stated for simplicity. In all instances, the words should be taken to refer to either gender.

Four words—Intelligence, Source, Essence and It—are sometimes capitalized to designate reference to *Thought* and the Greater Intelligence.

Chapter 1

The Experience of Illumination

A miracle is a beneficial phenomenon that is difficult to explain.

MRU

What is meant by Illumination? The word has several definitions and usages which do not apply here. As a capitalized word I use it as a name for the instance of experiencing the total unity of all that exists, without reference to any religion or philosophic view. Illumination is a brief elevated state of consciousness with the recipient losing all awareness of physical surroundings, including one's own body, and no sense of ego. There is only immaterial consciousness; self-identity as we recognize it is irrelevant. In this state, the sense of self-individuality is replaced by the experience of unity with the Intelligence that composes the physical universe and all therein. There is still personal awareness, but nothing distinct like a form or spirit body; no point of reference; nothing to distinguish oneself from the whole, other than a feeling of being melded with this whole.

This should not be confused with other types of inspiring psychic experiences. Having a sudden burst of insight into some matter or issue is a form of enlightenment, but is not indicative of the greater Illumination. A definition is one thing, but a description can be quite another. The following paragraphs give an idea of what the actual experience is like.

Illumination does not come at a time of one's own choosing; it can probably occur anytime and anyplace, provided that the person is somewhat relaxed mentally and physically—not necessarily intentionally relaxing, but rather in a passive state of mind. The experience begins without any indication of its coming and ends just as suddenly, with an extremely brief duration. The impression and feeling during the experience is like the merging of oneself (one's Self) with a greater Intelligence—that it was granted by an Intelligence greater than Self. This Greater Intelligence, as I choose to call it, has opened the mind of the recipient to perceive, feel and become conscious of existence when stripped from physical form and physical surroundings. It is a momentary departure from reality as we know it with no physical references whatsoever, no sense of place or time, no personal ego—only pure consciousness or awareness with what we call *thought*. This is not a psychic experience, which has more to do with the mind alone—this is of the Self, the spirit, the consciousness that a person is. There is no separation between this Intelligence and oneself; yet, one is greater than the other. Whatever one chooses to call the essence of this Intelligence, it is felt to be the source and guiding force of all that exists, whether physical or metaphysical. Nothing exists outside of this Essence. It *is* all that is—literal totality; not something just "out there", but within oneself as well. There is no sense of other identities—only this Greater Intelligence and one's own consciousness without the trivial concerns of earthly matters. The sense of human individuality is now combined with a known unity with this Intelligence and totality.

As awareness returns to one's physical surroundings there is a flood of emotions: ecstasy, awe, elation, love, humility, gratitude...; absolutely nothing that is of what we call a negative nature. The mind becomes a swirling mix of coherent thoughts to absorb and accept the change that has taken place in oneself as a result of this expanded consciousness. This is no mere intellectual or psychic experience, but a true life-experience. There is an overwhelming profound sense of peace in learning the true nature of Self. Life is *thought*; physical death is not an end, but merely a change, for there is no end to *thought*. *Thought* is ageless, boundless and formless. Behind the appearances of the physical universe, everything is one. Even with desire and an open mind for unknown knowledge the depth, intensity and impact of this experience are more than can be imagined.

Attaching words to what is felt and thought includes both questions and their answers for such an unanticipated surprising experience. "Wow! What just happened? Amazing! Incredible! I would never have guessed...! The answer to my prayers." And so on. This was part of my reaction as someone unfamiliar with even the idea of what a higher consciousness is or means. For anyone with some familiarity of this topic a forthcoming experience should be just as amazing, but less surprising, except perhaps for the intensity.

As self-identity is reasserted the impact of this experience sets in. It instantly gives the recipient a new perspective of life with knowledge and comprehension unlike that gained from conventional learning. This is life—existence—at its core. It is most profound and ecstatic! Nothing else can compare to it. This is a natural experience within human nature and is not dependent on any particular belief system. Although this elevated state of consciousness is fleeting (the duration is a mere instant, hardly even seconds at most), its effect on a person is permanent and is actually the next stage of personal evolution beyond consciousness of self. In the 19th century, Dr. Richard M. Bucke experienced Illumination and originated a term to refer to this stage that is still used today—Cosmic Consciousness.

The impact and effect of this experience cannot be overemphasized. It will change one's entire perspective of life in the physical world. Having briefly experienced non-dimensional consciousness, life and the universe are then seen in a whole different way. The nature and core of everything is *Thought*. The physical universe and all life therein are the embodiment, or manifestation, of this universal *Thought* within. The human Self is a part of the whole—everything is integrated. The Greater Intelligence is not just "out there", but is within as well. This is not comparable to an intellectual understanding of the concept—it is experiencing it, feeling it beyond our physical senses, momentarily becoming one with it (consciously, that is, for this is our nature, regardless of a lack of awareness of it). The influx of knowledge is tremendous. The feeling immediately following Illumination is that it is like acquiring years of study instantly, but with a significant difference. Unlike intellectual study in which information must be committed to memory, the recipient gains understanding and comprehension without the use of language or imagery. Whether that knowledge is somewhat familiar or entirely new, there is conviction in its validity and truth. Unlike our normal mental processing of one thought at a time, everything is simultaneous here. All that is learned during Illumination is instantly ingrained in the Self because it has been experienced, not studied.

To observe one's physical surroundings (including one's own body) at this moment is to see it all with "new eyes"; a door has been opened to experience true nature, thus giving vision for what the eyes cannot see. Visually, everything is the same as before, but perceptually, it all feels different—inwardly greatly more expansive. There is a new and deep respect for the world and all lifeforms. For the recipient, this is truly the day that the universe changed (in terms of awareness, that is). When looking around, the world is no longer composed of physical objects alone—there is the essence (the *thought*) that makes them what they are. Inhabiting a human body no longer gives a feeling of isolation (of individuality)—there is a relation of one-ness (more than a mere unity of individuals) with the world and the universe. There is absolutely no doubt about any of this—it is not a matter of belief or reasoning. The change of consciousness from isolated individual to integral union with the whole of existence is a stark contrast, rather like a demarcation line in one's life.

The body is seen for what it is—a marvelous organic machine, a tool for our use. It is the *thought*, the spirit-identity inside, that is the person. Instead of seeing oneself as the body, the spirit is more like a pilot or driver that is integrated with it.

What was gained in that instant makes it necessary to revise what was previously believed about reality to accommodate what lies behind and within the physical forms. From this day forward, the recipient will live his life based on this new perspective and has a personal challenge to describe it in language.

Aftermath

The oneness that is experienced is felt all the time along with having a serene inner peace. This is not just a realization of some new concept or the acquisition of a broad perception of reality. The expansion of consciousness was and is amazing for giving so much more than what had been hoped for.

In the ensuing weeks and months following Illumination, the recipient will feel an intense affinity with other lifeforms. Beyond the need for survival, which requires the taking of animal and plant life, there is empathy and intense sympathy regarding cruelty to (and the unnecessary suffering of) other creatures. This, of course, can be felt by anyone, but now is felt from a deeper awareness of spiritual relationships.

Among humans, though, there can be a feeling of loneliness if no one can be found who can relate to what had been experienced. There is an urge to share what was experienced with others whenever an opportunity presents itself, but that can initially be a mistake. I, myself, most often encountered quizzical facial expressions (as though my thinking had taken a weird twist) when trying to share some bits of the experience with friends and acquaintances. With those and similar reactions, a recipient may very quickly learn to be quiet about the matter and be selective about who to open up to. In my case, even years later stating or implying that such a grand experience had been had could be met with skepticism by some who had known me for any great length of time. Fortunately, nowadays (in the 2010s) this subject matter seems to be becoming generally more acceptable for ordinary conversation.

Since Illumination is an experience of the spirit, other people might associate it with religion. History is replete with individuals claiming divine revelations and communications with gods or God, adding to the myriad of religions and cults; such should not be the case here, though. The quest for Illumination should have no leaders and followers, only advisors and seekers.

Some might wonder if this is perhaps the workings of one's imagination. Others can and should be skeptical of things that are so very different from normal occurrences and that offer no material proof, but should also be open-minded enough to consider the possibilities. This makes it a question of belief—is it real or not? Are the recipients credible? If normally credible, could they be fooled by some trick of the mind? These are questions that the recipient must ask of himself as well. Days and weeks after the experience, the recipient should seek personal validation of it through self-analysis. Just some of the questions that can be asked of oneself are as follows: Was it genuinely real? Could it have been spontaneously imagined? It has changed my outlook of life, the world and the universe—is it for the better? Was it genuine Illumination, something lesser or a distortion? What were the physical conditions and state of mind immediately before and during the experience? Are there any negative effects on myself or other people as I interact with them? The recipient will also be curious about how his experience compares with that of others who claim to have experienced Illumination. Again, he may feel that no personal validation is necessary, but it should be sought to avoid being self-fooled.

Self-analysis isn't just to determine if it was real or not, it also helps to identify the degree of the experience. When a person experiences something extraordinary that gives beneficial insight and/or knowledge, it can be a major event in that person's life with perhaps a permanent effect. This is great for inner development and the evolution of consciousness and should not be downplayed by others. However, problems can arise if that experience is mistakenly identified as something greater than it is. If that happens, the error in identification and judgment might be passed on to others who accept it. Furthermore, depending on the person's frame of mind, it can potentially inflate the ego. It is necessary to closely examine and assess any personal extraordinary event for what it actually is. What is learned through Illumination must definitely be shared with others, but what is gained through inspiration or lesser enlightenment might be applicable only to oneself.

A Challenge to Share

There is a strong desire to share the knowledge that is gained with others, but the choice of terminology and the manner of presenting it are difficult to determine. The knowledge comes in a state that I call raw thought, because it is a comprehension of things disassociated from language and images. The recipient can easily apply this knowledge to his own life, but presenting it to others is a whole other matter. On one hand, there is the unity of everything at the metaphysical level; on the other hand, there is the distinctness, or separateness, of everything at the physical level. Metaphysically, all is one and one is all; physically, the individuality of forms predominates. To the recipient this unity is simplicity itself, despite the complexity of physical forms and properties.

It is the difficult task of a recipient to convert this profound non-dimensional experience into concepts that non-recipients might possibly be able to relate to intellectually. However a recipient chooses to describe

Illumination, it should not be forced into the framework of any particular belief system for that would take much away from its overall significance. It is one thing to use language and concepts that are familiar to oneself and others, but quite another thing to insist that it is only that way. Although the concepts presented will naturally and unavoidably be influenced by the recipients' cultural background, so that descriptions may vary widely, the root message of the unity of all things and all life should be intact. I try to convey the simplicity of unity by not over-categorizing things. Regardless of any intellectual description, though, words do not do justice to the experience itself.

In attempting to relate the experience for others the recipient becomes acutely aware of the limitations of our communicative tools, which are basically language, art and music. Each can be used to present aspects to different effect, but none are entirely satisfactory—language is more technical and can deal with specifics, whereas art and music can more easily touch the emotions, but are more subject to viewer and listener interpretations. The great tragedy of language, though, is that it is easy to pick apart statements word by word that can detract from intent and meaning or to over-interpret them. A speaker or writer might use words that seem clear and appropriate at the time, but are later seen to be open to unintended interpretations. How common it is for a speaker's words to be challenged and then defended by saying "That's not what I meant". A writer has the advantage of having more time to consider the choice of words, but still cannot foresee every possible misunderstanding from what is meant. In contrast, art and music are not subject to this type of criticism because any intended message is left to the mind of the individual viewer/listener to discover.

To reiterate, Illumination is a brief expansion of consciousness into the core of reality, which is nonphysical, non-imaged and non-symbolic. Experiencing the unity of totality should not be confused with a realm of countless individual spirits and a hierarchy of entities. Unity and individuality can be likened to flip sides of the same coin—one side represents true nature and the other represents the forms and aspects of manifestations. Everything is of the same essence, but seen from two different perspectives.

The earlier statement that "it is like acquiring years of study instantly" requires some clarification. It is not an acquisition of knowledge of subjects per se, but a metaphysical perspective of existence that relates spiritual actuality to physical reality from which knowledge is derived. The matter at hand here is how a person perceives and understands the nature and interrelationships of all that he encounters. Consider how many years it takes a human child to learn about the world in which he lives and how to interact with it. From birth to near adolescence, he builds a perspective of physical reality through experience and aid from parents and teachers that is continually improved and refined into adulthood. Now imagine compressing those years into a fleeting second or so. What one has is instant perception and perspective that can only come from a source outside of oneself.

Because all was learned simultaneously, the recipient sees the interconnectedness and wants to convey this to others, but language permits only linear descriptions. Therefore, it is necessary for the reader to visualize a whole from the various parts and to not take those parts out of context from the whole.

How can there be more than a modicum of description of a perspective of life, whether physical or metaphysical? How can this all be shared without sounding self-important or immodest, as though having privileged information? There is no vanity here, no wish for undue attention—only a sincere desire to assist fellow mankind in personal development by speaking from an uncommon perspective. The knowledge gained must certainly be shared (not kept to oneself and lost to others) even if only a small number of individuals may benefit from it, but it is more important to stress the reality of Illumination and encourage others to strive for the experience themselves. If some of the content herein sounds disagreeable to one's experiences in life, then take that as a challenge to encourage personal thought and contemplation for things that are currently unknown or unproven to oneself, instead of rejecting things outright without consideration.

Reflecting on Universal Unity

Even after the passing of decades, the effects of this experience do not fade with time as though it relied on memory alone, because it is the spirit that is affected. In living with the perspective of total metaphysical unity it becomes increasingly rather difficult to remember one's previous perspective prior to the point of Illumination; that is, of being a lone physical individual consciously isolated from the whole. There might have been (or might be for others) a subjective feeling of connection with other people or with nature in general, but it was/is based on the distinctiveness that is inherent in self-consciousness, i.e., individuality. To exemplify this, I regularly recall the moments in which my perspective was forever altered—not to reminisce the ecstasy that followed as though to mentally repeat it, rather, to not forget how it felt to be conscious only of Self in the preceding moments. After experiencing the unified nature of existence, the perception of life through only individuality becomes just a memory.

Chapter 2

The Greater Intelligence

The One is all things and not a single one of them...
Plotinus, Ennead V-2-1

What term can be used to refer to an intelligent entity that is within all matter and spirit? From religions, myths and some philosophies there are numerous names and terms for a supreme entity or ultimate cause of existence, but nearly all are derived from the perspective of distinct individual self-conscious beings and so reflect that separateness in body and spirit. However, the higher consciousness experienced through Illumination demonstrates that *thought* is the foundation of totality. No single word is more descriptive than that, so I use the capitalized, italicized word *'Thought'* rather than existing terms that have established meanings and connotations.

Thought is what composes the universe. It is a conscious intelligence that *is* the nature and core of totality, the driving force that evolves the universe, maintaining order according to It's design. This

Thought should not be likened to limited human thought for it has no ego, no petty concerns that are inherent in individual lifeforms. *Thought* feels through emotions, but can have no vices unto Itself for It is totality, which has no ego. *Thought* has no origin Itself, but is the origin and essence of all that is. Before the existence of the physical universe, there was only *Thought*. Without matter, even space did not exist for there were no points of reference. Neither were there spirits, no distinctions of any kind whatsoever—only *Thought*. This was a true void. By the creative power and energy of thought alone, *Thought* caused to initiate the formation of physical matter and their properties that set into motion all the actions and reactions that came to form the universe. Those properties include the natural forces that established order in the young cosmos early on. As an Intelligence, *Thought* equates to order—It's will to manifest and express in material forms necessitates it. If there was any chaos, it lasted only until there was sufficient matter for mutual reactions to give celestial shape to stellar and interstellar bodies. Thus, the universe is a manifestation of *Thought's* desire to express It's inherent creative nature. This self-expression of *Thought* is an on-going process of change that is determinative, but subtle and slow acting; slow by human perception, not when considering infinite time. However subtle, it is a driving force that never lets up—a desire to develop, improve and refine the means of expression.

As to how *Thought* formed the initial matter and set the universe in motion, that remains a mystery. All matter is imbued with *Thought* and every piece of matter, from the sub-atomic level on up, has varying degrees of intelligence according to its ability to express *Thought*. Inorganic, inanimate matter, though, has limited possibilities for expression after their properties have been established and is at a level so low that we do not acknowledge it for practical purposes. For example, celestial bodies act on and react to other bodies in accordance with physical forces in which there is no apparent decision making to alter their courses through space, with the same being true for planetary environments. They seemingly do what they do by design alone. And there it is...order by intelligent design.

For direct expression of *Thought's* creativity a means of animating matter was and is needed. The development of organic life allows greater and finer expression of *Thought*, but it came with autonomy for the organisms; i.e., the ability to make decisions apart from the whole solely for its own physical form. This physical distinction caused a loss of awareness of *Thought* by organisms despite being one with It. In other words, the rise of autonomous individual intelligence in the physical realm had the unfortunate consequence of losing awareness of the Greater Intelligence within.

In a nutshell, such is the basis of how the universe came to be, which necessarily sounds like myth. A somewhat expanded version of this follows in the subsections below to give a better idea of how *Thought's* expression is accomplished. Though theoretical in detail by having been surmised from both a physical perspective and that which was gained from Illumination, it is accurate in principle to show the interconnectedness and interplay of spirit (specifically the controlling intelligence) with organic matter regardless of the actual method. Furthermore, the distinction between the aforementioned terms '*Thought*' and 'Greater Intelligence' must be made clear and will be dealt with incrementally.

Aside from a mythical sounding story, what is *Thought*? To answer that question fairly, it is necessary for the reader to set aside ideas about egos and individuality and be open to consider a unified perspective of existence. However, everything that is examined or considered is inevitably placed within some context of personal experience and what is understood or believed to be true about reality. Reason and logic can be used to some effect to obtain a neutral attitude, but logic is limited to the sensibleness derived from one's own experiences. Concepts that are outside of one's logic are easy to reject and this is where having an open mind helps to cope with what is personally unknown.

Thought is responsible for all that exists, but is no god or deity because It *is* all that exists. For humans to conceive a God or gods is understandable, though, from the perspective of individuality that comes with self-consciousness. There is oneself inhabiting one body that is distinct from other objects and entities and we necessarily live our lives according to this outlook. Any feeling or sense of an intelligence or power to explain the creation of the universe is understandably perceived as something distinct and greater than ourselves. But, from a perspective of consciousness that is higher than self, any term used for *Thought* to signify supremacy should be relative to all forms being integral with the whole, not with natures being distinct or separate.

Thought is an intelligent, conscious ethereal essence that manifested to form matter by sheer will alone. This was not instantaneous creation of a formed universe, rather a process of ongoing intelligent, progressive development. Everything that exists, including life, is of that essence. There is no separation, no distinction in nature, only distinction in physical forms. In a manner of speaking, *Thought* is the original artist, designer and sculptor (or engineer, draftsman and builder) of the universe. Using material of It's own formation, It made the universe what it is and continues to shape and refine that expression, but the progression from initial desire to what exists today was not preordained—it will always be a work in progress.

Prior to experiencing the higher consciousness that comes with Illumination, the totality that is *Thought* is not something that can be easily related to. With limited perception, perspective and consciousness, a practical approach to *Thought* must be narrowed. Consequently, by default we humans have historically sought an intelligence outside of ourselves that is responsible for creation—I call this the Greater Intelligence (G.I.).

The G.I. as a term is narrowed to refer specifically to the guiding intelligence (the principle aspect) of *Thought,* particularly as it applies to lifeforms. It is subliminal in the mental makeup of every living thing—unrealized, but there. Mankind, however, as a highly evolved form, has the ability for every individual to eventually attain that personal realization. The relationship between the G.I. and a lifeform's relative individual intelligence residing within the same physical body is best described by an analogy using the human body.

The body is composed of a great many individual cells united in a manner to give a specific form. Cells of each type join to form the various body parts and the individual cells within those types have a function to do. Every cell is a life onto itself with enough intelligence to fulfill its purpose and cooperate with other cells for the good of the whole body, in effect making it a small universe of cells functioning autonomically. The human spirit resides within the body of cells, but not in any particular organ or area exclusively; it is within every cell without occupying space. It can be said that the spirit is kind of like in the background of each cell even if the cells are unaware of it. In a manner of speaking, the individual cell's intelligence is considered to be local and the intelligence of the human spirit is bodily universal. Although the cells are only concerned with their own functions they are integral with the whole. The human spirit can readily control movement of the body as a whole and can affect specific parts (essentially large groups of cells) by concentrating thoughts on them, although singling-out individual cells may well be beyond our present ability. In effect, there are two levels of intelligence within the cells that are co-mingled. The cells do not need direct assistance from the human spirit to perform their functions, but without the presence of the spirit all the cells die (although they can be kept alive for some time artificially). Similarly, the human spirit does not need a body of cells for continuous existence, but the body is needed for self-expression.

Each and every cell is a life itself with the conglomerate giving form for the expression of a greater (take that as more evolved or developed) spirit-identity. This is the same principle, but on a smaller scale, as *Thought* manifesting in the universe.

Consciousness permeates the body just as the G.I. permeates all matter.

We humans are like cells that can feel or sense an intelligence greater than our own, but typically seek it outside of ourselves. Hence, we have a multitude of ideas and beliefs in mythologies, religions and philosophies regarding the nature of existence, commonly having a god or gods. However, as the consciousness of Man evolves, he comes to see that the G.I. is within the self as well as all around.

There will never be an adequate or satisfactory description of the relationships and interactions between lifeforms, the world environment, the universe and the G.I. This is the nature of totality, of individuals united in the whole as one. Much of what is stated in this section defies the ordinary experience of daily life and is easy to dismiss if it cannot be related to. Even so, attempts at description must be made despite the inherent difficulties. As previously stated, the only evidence for any of this is in the testaments of recipients themselves and the only proof is in experiencing Illumination for oneself. I suggest comparing the contents of this book with the writings of other purported genuine recipients to discern common elements regardless of the terminology used or descriptions given. Also (and most importantly), seek Illumination for oneself.

Development of Organic Expression

[This and all the following sub-sections use both past and present tenses to denote that the fundamental processes that initiate and evolve life are unchanged and still on-going.]

With an orderly, dynamic universe established a special type of matter capable of animation had to be developed that would become the foundation and avenue for *Thought's* direct creative expression at local levels, although how this was initially done remains another mystery. The formation of the first functioning organic matter that we call single cellular life included autonomy to act on *Thought's* inherent desire to manifest, meaning that they could adapt to conditions for survival and replicate or reproduce for continued existence, which is their only directive. These adaptive cells became the basic building block material for multicellular forms with increasing complexity that allowed for the extraordinary development of spirits. Multiple cells that cohered to make single larger forms need/needed a higher intelligence to oversee and direct the developing forms (in effect bringing order to them with the added directive to improve expression) which they in turn would cooperate with. At some indiscernible point at which the cell-forms need assistance guidance is provided by the G.I. through what immediately became spirits. [The consequence of this spiritual guidance is related in the following subsection.] In contrast to these tiny developing forms, colonies of cells that lack equivalent cohesion remain masses of independent individuals.

There are two related aspects of *Thought*—manifestation and expression—that are inherent in the nature of all organisms and dominate and drive their lives. Cells fulfill the drive to manifest and the ones that are in multicellular forms are dedicated to serving the needs of the higher intelligence (spirit) imbued within them. Cells are the machinery of organic life with a level of intelligence that is limited to single cell tasks and when they expire the animating force within them simply dissipates. Expression is carried out by the spirit within each multicellular body to oversee, direct and evolve those wonderfully adaptive cells into forms (meaning all the organs and features that compose them) that improve survival and ultimately lead to increasingly intelligent expressive capability by influencing all of them without being centered in any of them. In this way a spirit is not diminished when cells die, provided that vital parts of the forms remain functional. The decision making by spirits is what I call local intelligence because they are concerned specifically with the utilization of the bodies in their charge.

The desire of *Thought* to express necessitates ever-improving lifeforms striving for two key features that provide more versatility than do sedentary forms.

1) Mobility and the ability to manipulate objects in the environment. 2) Sufficient brain development to allow increasing levels of intelligence and consciousness. With this base directive, spirits evolve organisms into myriad forms and this will continue forever, striving to achieve combinations of physical dexterity with creative and imaginative intelligence.

Expression improves with experience and degrees of consciousness. What we call lower lifeforms may not express much beyond satisfying the drive to manifest, such as developing survival skills and reproducing, but higher forms can express in ways that go beyond those needs. Mammals in particular have a range of emotions that are expressed through their behavior and humans out-do all other known lifeforms with our creativity in the arts and ability to think abstractly.

Individual Lifeform Identities

It might help to think of those early multicellular forms as something like sensors and the spirits imbued in them as non-corporeal memory cells for the G.I. at a local level. The experience of living, of manipulating a body, of interacting with an environment and other organisms add to the cumulative memory of *Thought* as part of It's desire to express. However, the autonomy of a new spirit, coupled with its decision making being limited and dedicated to a single physical body concerned only with itself, created a sense of identity. Not like we typically think of it—just a sense of existing separate from the environment, of being an individual unit of something distinct from all other objects. The distinction between this identity and the G.I., however, is apparent only, not actual, but persisted even after the death of its physical host body. The experience of living garnered by a non-corporeal memory cell became more than a memory for *Thought*—it became like a life unto itself, an idea that clung to autonomy.

This little non-corporeal memory cell of identity retained the directive from the G.I. (to exist and express itself) as though it were its own, even after losing its physical host body through death. Here was the beginning of what we call a spirit. Originating as a form of expression of *Thought*, the spirit acquired, or assumed, the illusion of having a separate identity. The spirit's continued desire to express itself eventually allowed it to manifest again in another physical body, but this could be done only through the G.I. Although the spirit's illusory identity has the desire to manifest, it has no power to do so independently, but is allowed to because it still serves the whole that is *Thought*. Multiple successive manifestations of this non-corporeal memory cell (this spirit) served to effectively make it a seeming repository for specific life experiences, thus intensifying its sense of identity. Since each spirit develops into a unique set of life experiences, I use the term *spirit-identity* to refer to its individual sense of existence—its individuality. Whether or not the development of spirit-identities was intended, it was allowed to continue—and although a spirit-identity clings to its cumulative memories of experiences as its own, they are always within the whole of *Thought's* expressiveness. This is not saying that spirit-identities can recall memories of previous manifestations at will while incarnate, for that would be unnecessarily confusing without having the mental discipline to distinguish past-life memories from the present life.

For the tiniest lifeforms that are at the initial stage of receiving guidance from the G.I., not every incoming spirit will be the making of a new one because the drive and desire of existing spirit-identities for continued manifestation gives them priority with the G.I.

Evolving Expression

[For this sub-section, exclude any thought of homo sapiens.]

Lifeforms exist as a means for improved expression of *Thought*, even though the spirit-identities are unaware of this, being concerned only with their own physical existence and continuance. As a spirit-identity gains experience and learns from its cumulative manifestations, it gradually masters the use of the forms (or types of forms) that it had been inhabiting. When it does it can next manifest in a so-called higher form that will allow a greater degree of expression. If no higher form exists at that time, then it will have greater desire and drive in successive manifestations within existing forms to further aid their physical evolution. In other words, it must be thoroughly experienced in utilizing a type of form before advancing to another type that will allow greater physical and/or mental expression. The advancement between forms may be moderate or minute.

During this process there is a dual drive to improve the forms. First and foremost is the will of the G.I. to improve all lifeforms, which allow greater expression. Note that this is not a goal, for a goal marks the end of something; expression is never-ending and the possibilities are limitless. Second is the inherent desire of the spirit-identity to improve itself. These two associated drives together are responsible for the ongoing evolution of life and operate subliminally. One significant distinction between them is that the spirit-identity's desire for expression is limited to itself. There is no deliberate thought beyond surviving one single manifestation within the environment into which it is born, but this drive extends for a collective effect within any given species in which a spirit-identity finds itself. Thus, it is the collective spirit-identities that are most responsible for the specifics of physical organic evolution within a species as a whole, i.e., the shapes of bodies, their characteristics and behaviors.

We generally think of lifeforms as being lower or higher on a relative scale of intelligence. Lower forms typically display similar behaviors within the same species, while higher forms can have greater diversity between individuals. This is due to the variation and amount of cumulative life experiences among spirit-identities, with each striving to express itself. There is conformance to species behavior, but higher forms with more developed spirits allow a kind of personality, or disposition, to be expressed by individuals. As previously intimated, ideal forms for creative expression combine physical dexterity with brains that permit greater degrees of intelligence—and a balance between them has the most potential.

Opportunities for spirits to reincarnate depend on the availability of suitable forms and the intensity of their individual desire and drive to advance. Most opportunities to manifest are among the lower lifeforms (such as plants and insects for example) with their virtually limitless numbers through the ages. With comparatively lower populations of incrementally higher lifeforms, spirits do not all develop at the same rate. Some feel a greater desire to steadily advance while many are content to linger at some stage(s). Fluctuating populations, including extinctions, greatly affect the intervals between incarnations of any particular spirit and necessitate that the G.I. set priorities, considering all factors as they change, for the desirous and less desirous spirits to reincarnate, but should not be thought of as a ruler or judge making every decision for the reincarnation of every spirit every time. Spirits and the G.I. are aspects within the one-ness of *Thought* and the G.I. simply has a greater degree of influence for expressional needs/desires.

Through the eons of life on Earth, forms have come and gone with drastic changes to suit changing needs, but some have remained fundamentally unchanged for great lengths of time because they are so well suited for their roles in nature as well as their stages for mental development. Throughout all this, the trials and attempts of the G.I. and spirits to evolve forms that are suitable for greater mental potential and higher thinking eventually brought about one or more forms capable of realizing a higher degree of consciousness than the need for mere physical survival. Attaining consciousness of a spiritual self was a major advance for the expression of *Thought*.

Self-consciousness

All lifeforms have an inherent awareness of being distinct from other lifeforms, which gives them a limited sense of identity whether or not it is realized,

The Greater Intelligence

but when a spirit-identity has a realization that it can think in ways that go beyond the needs of survival and species interaction, of being an independent thinking and feeling (emotionally) individual, it will have become self-conscious. This in turn encourages self-interest and the further development of unique personalities. It is debatable whether or not homo sapiens are the only species that have attained this state because certain other species certainly show characteristics of unique personality among individuals that go beyond survival and play. However, we are handicapped in efforts to communicate and learn what those creatures think and feel. It is important not to think of humanity as being so far removed from the animal kingdom simply because our mental capacity and intellect are apparently so much greater than theirs.

What really sets humans apart on the evolutionary ladder of Earth is our ability to introspect. Introspection permits free and abstract thinking. It is this that opens the mind to seek to understand personal identity and how it relates to the world, besides understanding the functioning of our physical environment as far as we can perceive. Identity itself is an abstract (or spiritual) thing that can engender acceptance of other spiritual entities. From that came attempts in ancient times to understand and explain the forces of nature and man's position through mythology, progressing to religions, philosophies and sciences.

Although certain animal species demonstrate varying degrees of intelligence, only humans can think abstractly to the best of our knowledge, which puts us at the present pinnacle of organic and psychic evolution on Earth. We have the greatest potential to express various aspects of the G.I. by striving to live by ideals that can improve our understanding of and relationships with each other. However, free thinking also allows thoughts of selfishness and all the vices that come with and from that. The potential problem here is in how an individual chooses to deal with the ego in relation to other people and lifeforms. Spirit-identities inhabiting human form are so varied in development that behavioral extremes of vice and virtue with everything in between are found among us.

Behaviors can be taught, encouraged and forced upon us by others, but are ultimately personal choices. Each of us has a guide that can help to steer us toward what is right and good in our interactions with each other and other lifeforms if a person will listen to it—we call this guide *conscience* and it is actually the G.I. within us. Conscience often teaches its lessons after decisions are carried out by giving feelings of satisfaction or regret, but unfortunately some people have numbed themselves to disregard the conscience wholly or in part.

With all the potential that self-consciousness allows for personal expression, it is still limited to the self—

the individual. Everything that is perceived, determined and surmised is from an individual (physically and spiritually) point of view. As a spirit-identity progresses through the experiences of multiple manifestations in human form, learning to improve and refine it's perspective of self and the physical environment (including other lifeforms), it eventually reaches a point of readiness to accept a higher degree of consciousness.

Cosmic Consciousness

Attaining this stage of consciousness takes the recipient beyond the individual to experience the unity of all things in one behind the forms of the physical universe. It is a vastly expanded degree of awareness that the recipient permanently retains following Illumination. Although there can be more than one instance of this experience by an individual, each is brief, but with a permanent effect. Note that it is not a *state* of Illumined consciousness that is permanent, but rather its effect of expanded awareness and comprehension that remains active with the recipient.

This state is totally non-dimensional without images or symbols and there is no sense of personal identity or other entities. Significantly, there is no personal dynamic thinking (no control or direction of thought—only awareness) because all is one. Use of the phrase 'all is one' in this context aids in description, but implies a unity of separate entities when there is actually only One. This word or name (One), so to speak, was used by the 3rd century philosopher Plotinus and is just as appropriate as my use of *'Thought'*. There are only aspects of *Thought* without any distinctions, thus having all potentialities. Being conscious of this oneness but having no control might seemingly imply at least a duality, for would a recipient not be something like an observer? This, however, is not what is felt. Oneself is not just a part of this whole and the word 'integral' is not exactly suitable either, because it still implies some kind of distinction. Even 'oneself' is not appropriate because there is no sense of Self. There is only one aspect that comes close to being a distinction when compared with personal awareness and that is the G.I., the guiding Intelligence aspect of *Thought*. The difference is in dynamics. The G.I. is active dynamic thinking, whereas personal awareness is passive and impassive. This, however, has significance only when consciousness returns to the physical realm (or a realm of forms, be they material or spiritual) and active thinking is regained.

Having experienced an absence of other identities in this state does not mean that there is an exalted or otherwise special status for oneself in life. It represents a conscious return to origin, which every spirit eventually reaches. Illumination is all about learning of our nature as expressive agents of *Thought* and applying that knowledge in life. Although having identities is useful and even necessary in a material realm where individuality is inherent, they mean nothing when there is only *Thought* without manifested expression.

Having this expanded perspective does not have to change one's activities or type of work occupation. This is just the beginning of contemplating how to use a physical body (in present and future incarnations anywhere in the universe) for joint cooperative expression with the G.I. Although the spirit-identity continues to predominate the use of physical forms, being aware that all that we experience and all that we feel emotionally are part of the whole makes a recipient a more cooperative agent of expression.

Illumination provides so much that one instance is sufficient for the remainder of one's life. There is no need for a repeat of the same experience, because this is an evolution of consciousness, not education. The effects of experiencing conscious union with universal *Thought* do not fade with time and this maintains an inner serenity for the recipient regardless of difficulties in life. Any successive experience of Illumination will enhance or expand on the first as a supplement without repeating it.

There is good reason why experiencing Illumination is brief. We exist physically as autonomous expressions of *Thought* so consciousness is tied to the body (or based in the body) for its duration. Since Illumination momentarily moves conscious awareness away from both physical and spiritual forms entirely, there is no feeling of one's social identity and no personal control or direction of thought because all is one—keep in mind that this is non-dimensional. In this state there is no activity for there is nothing to act upon; no means of expression, therefore no creativity; no emotions other than a serene peace; no sense of time for there are no points of reference. When consciousness is regained in the physical body one's thinking becomes active again and is supplemented with this expansive perspective of nature. There should be no desire to repeat and prolong genuine Illumination because it serves no practical purpose. Furthermore, prolongation implies a sense of time, which means mixed aspects of physical and metaphysical properties and dimension, thus making it a different kind of experience.

Being in this non-dimensional state is basically emotionless compared to how we feel emotions in life, for they are a serene whole without an ego to see them separately or selectively. Emotions that can rise and fall are felt only upon the return of consciousness to the body. The flood of them that accompany a first experience do so because of the tremendous impact that it makes in the mind in this physical realm; successive instances can leave different impacts. It is a mistake for anyone to think of Illumination as a state or condition of bliss.

As a recipient applies this expanded view of existence to his life, there is a chance of expanding it further with more Illumination if and when he is ready and whether or not a supplement will be helpful for his continuing work. As always, there should be no expectation of receiving it, but remain open-minded for whatever may come.

The number of incarnations necessary for a spirit-identity to evolve to this point of readiness is different for every individual. The variables are the virtually unlimited life-decisions that each spirit makes throughout all previous lifetimes. Basically, decisions that are beneficial for the progressive expressions of the G.I. (even though unknown to an individual) aid the development of Self, whereas ones that are made of a purely selfish nature are detrimental and slow one's spiritual growth.

Having this higher degree of consciousness, though, does not free a recipient from the trials, tribulations and temptations of life. Life continues as before with the same potential for all things—for both beneficence as well as misery. Despite the great change in awareness and perception of existence, the pressures of life on oneself do not change. One is still subject to making mistakes, making good and bad judgment calls, suffering from disease, and so on. Furthermore, the recipient can still potentially backslide into selfish acts, but I think that is unlikely on more than a tiny scale, because he will want to prevent any backsliding. Despite these continuing trials in life with sometimes unpleasant or undesirable emotions there is the serene inner peace within oneself that never goes away.

At this level there is some amount of conscious influence over one's next incarnation in the way of choice. Unless a recipient makes some kind of big blunder or the expressive needs of the G.I. overrule personal desires, the recipient can choose to return to Earth or move on to another stage elsewhere in the universe for other types of expression. This is why there will never be a predominance of cosmic conscious individuals among humans on Earth, because at some point they *must* move on. The wide range within self-consciousness is necessary for a spirit to develop through it before attaining the cosmic level.

Devotion to the G.I.

The preceding sections of this chapter describing *Thought* and manifestation may sound totally impersonal with no room for love of a God as found in religions. Actually, love for the Intelligence that formed the universe is deepened through greater appreciation for the interconnectedness of everything and the realization of one's role in it. The flood of emotions that come following Illumination is indeed very personal and part of the experience, with the first occurrence of it being like a grand homecoming with love all around. Experiencing the unity of all things shows the blending of the personal and impersonal aspects of *Thought*.

For a non-recipient, a Creator God is typically felt or perceived as being either personal or impersonal depending on which aspects are dominant in one's thinking. For simplicity, the physical universe and its natural forces can be associated with impersonal aspects, while the G.I. is associated with personal ones that man can interact with intellectually and emotionally. Note that my reference is to *aspects*—not to an actual impersonal entity that created the universe and its order only to leave it alone, neither to a personal entity that is something like an omnipotent and all-knowledgeable person. Love is inherent in the G.I. and can be felt by anyone who is open to it. It is the G.I. (under any other name) that is prayed to and supplicated for succor. [Another note: This is not worship—it is reverence for the root intelligence (the Source) of the whole of existence of which we are a small part.] A recipient differs from others by relating to the G.I. in all aspects of *Thought*, not exclusively to personal or impersonal ones. Love, admiration, awe and reverence extend to all of nature universally.

Following Illumination, prayer takes on even more meaning and significance than before. Praying to the G.I. will become more like communing, if it wasn't before. Emotions, desires and other feelings (i.e., raw thoughts before they are put into words) can be more intense and honest than words can convey, so words are not necessary. Prayers do not need to be verbal unless participating in group prayer for others to share in the same thoughts. In my case, I surmised this in my youth and it was validated through this experience.

More on Personal Identity and Expression

As mentioned in the sub-section *Individual Lifeform Identities* in this chapter, spirits think that they are distinct from *Thought* because of their autonomous behavior and sense of identity being coupled with a necessarily distinct physical body. This is the great illusion in life—that of being a truly distinct, fully separate entity. In contrast, though, it is also said by some others that life itself is an illusion—that physical reality is not truly real, that it is only virtual. The definitions of and differences between reality and illusion can be debated endlessly philosophically, scientifically and psychologically, but we still have to cope and interact with the here and now in a practical sense regardless of what is thought about it. Whether incarnate or disembodied, spirits cling to distinctions until reaching Illumination, which temporarily subsumes identity within the oneness of true nature. When this is experienced identities are accepted as necessary classifications for interaction in this physical realm, but no longer as truly separate entities. So long as spirits continue to serve the purpose of *Thought's* expressiveness and meet the practical needs of being in a physical environment a sense of identity will be retained. To put it another way, realizing the illusory perception of identity does not negate its usefulness.

Regarding human spirits specifically as advanced Earthly agents of expression for *Thought* I feel that Illumination marks the apex of what can be attained spiritually on Earth, but it definitely is not the end of spiritual evolution. Illumination is just the beginning of the next level of consciousness that we call Cosmic. The spirit-identity that reaches it is somewhat comparable to a school graduate that is ready to apply what has been learned and is willing to go wherever he may be useful or needed in future incarnations. He may reincarnate on Earth as a teacher to further assist spiritually inclined individuals or move on for other forms of expression. It is neither my feeling nor opinion that a spirit-identity can reach a point of not having to reincarnate (or manifest in some type of form that is capable of manipulating matter) because that is in opposition to the drive of *Thought* to manifest and It's directive to continually refine expression, both of which are innate within every spirit. To many individuals this might be an unwelcome thought because there seems to be no goal, no end to it, but that is due to the limited perspective of self-consciousness. The G.I. has no predetermined universal objective—only continual creative expression with infinite possibilities. Does an artist ever stop being an artist—thinking like an artist? Is a true artist ever fully satisfied with every detail of a supposed completed work? For such an individual, satisfaction only means accepting that it is the best that he could do at a given time. So it is with the G.I. working through us and other evolving lifeforms in a never ending process of refinement.

Regardless of an individual's stage of spiritual development our role in this is fulfilled simply through our own self-expression. Enjoy life through activities that are generally benign, bringing pleasure and satisfaction without being harmful to or derisive of others, neither being wantonly destructive. This applies to everything that we do, including our methods and means of survival, and has behavioral constraints (both specified and implied) that are expounded in our vast arrays of civic laws and codes of ethics to encourage peaceful and orderly coexistence.

Formlessness

Although it should be apparent by now, it is worth emphasizing that the immateriality that is experienced with Illumination is not at all like the spiritual realm in which disembodied spirits reside, having a sometimes-visible form without physicality or such as are reported by many individuals who have had near-death or out-of-body experiences. There are not even thought-images, which would imply spacial reference, for this is non-dimensional. Any kind of non-physical experience that retains a sense of identity, form, dimension, time or allows individual dynamic thinking is something else that is not relevant here. The point being made is that genuine Illumination that takes us consciously into the state of our originating source differs from all other experiences.

This non-dimensional experience is essentially devoid of distinctions, but does not feel like a void. The essence of all things manifested are felt to be present and in one (i.e., One)—there is no feeling of absence. The ethereal conglomerate that makes up totality is so thoroughly mixed that it is something like an immaterial puree of aspects. Consciousness does not actually go anywhere, but rather is expanded (or opened) to become aware of this unity, this one-ness. Immediately following Illumination, there is no sense or thought of mental images or symbols—nothing that is representative, for that creates distinctions, which detracts from one-ness.

Chapter 3

Advice for the Seeker

Before criticizing others one should first look at oneself with the same scrutiny.
(A variation of the Bible's Matthew 7:3-5) MRU

There are undoubtedly numerous methods professed by individuals and organizations to direct seekers toward higher consciousness and Illumination, but how effective any of them may be (including what I suggest) depends on the present state of inner development of any given seeker and the degree of commitment. The choice of what method to use should be a matter of what can best be related to. I can state only what worked for me and what can be determined to be generally valid regardless of what other method may be used.

It was only in retrospective thought that I could state specifically what practices of mine helped lead to the experience that answered my long-standing questions about life. The following subsections represent what I practiced in my youth and early adult life and continue to practice. The one exception to this is the subsection *Spirit and Body,* which I began immediately after experiencing Illumination.

The effectiveness of any method depends on how much effort is put into it, but my suggestions should be easy to incorporate into one's life. My recommendations are few, but need to be practiced persistently. It is not necessary to take time away from other activities or to change one's lifestyle. Almost all effort put into this quest is mental and emotional that can be practiced almost anytime, anyplace. The few exercises that I recommend (in *Spirit and Body*) can be done when going to bed, if at no other time. The objective is to keep certain ideas and desires active in the mind so that they become routine and constant regardless of whatever else one may be doing. When they become routine, then they have advanced the Self and are no longer merely thoughts in the mind. There should be no conflict if choosing to combine some or all of my suggestions with other methods.

Regardless of methods and practices used by others, the quest for Illumination is ultimately and necessarily personal. Following the advice of others does not mean to be a "follower" of the person giving it. Such advice is intended (or should be intended) only to assist the seeker in his personal effort toward self-improvement and understanding. There is no guarantee of attaining Illumination with any method. This is not like an instructional science lab project that will give known results immediately after having done certain things. Patience and perseverance are key—think long-term. Even if higher consciousness is not reached, achieving various other insights along the way will show that progress will have been made.

Imagine that the knowledge that is sought is to be found at the peak of a moderate size mountain that must be climbed all alone. Standing near the base you see that it is covered with trees and shrubs, but has a few sparse areas. The peak has what appears to be a small plateau. Around the mid-section several trails can be seen through the foliage and nearer to the top at least one trail can be discerned. The base has a number of trailheads that allow an easy start and the slope all around the mountain gives the appearance of being not so strenuous for a hike. The few visible steep areas "can surely be avoided" is the thought that comes to mind. Many guides are available to help you get started and can join you for part of the way, but only general advice can be given for how to stay on one's chosen course and not stray. There is no map, no list of directions, and no set of instructions to follow for a guaranteed route. Every step of the way is a personal decision for what is needed at any given time. There will be obstacles, pauses, setbacks and advances. At times, you will find that the trail you were on has gradually ended and you must blaze your own way to get back on track. Whether following a trail that was advised by others or blazing a new one, it is the upward direction that must be maintained.

The analogy above is easy to visualize, unlike the effects of challenges that confront us in everyday life. A status check of whether or not progress is being made is in how one feels about oneself along the way. Situations and conditions that adversely affect one's outlook of life should not be dwelt on any longer than necessary, because they will slow or halt progress, even potentially causing regression.

Before proceeding, it must be understood that I assume a seeker to already have a concept and acceptance of some kind of Intelligence that is responsible for all that exists and it is not so important exactly how it is conceived or perceived. Being uncertain that such an Intelligence exists is okay, but to deny even the possibility is to deny the spiritual Self. Accepting the spirituality of life is requisite for all that I write. It is also helpful (but not necessary for the advice provided below) to be at least open-minded about the possibility that spirits are not limited to just one physical incarnation.

It all starts with pondering how life, the world and the universe came into existence and why. Aside from the physical forms, what is the nature of life? What is the meaning of it all? Who and what am I and why am I here? Many more questions progress from these and there are no generally accepted answers. Religions and philosophies provide world-views and belief systems that satisfy a great many people, but with each claiming to have or know "the truth", what really is the truth about life and existence? Source material is all-important in any kind of research and applies equally to the origin of beliefs, but what does one do when there are multiple sources with conflicting information and interpretations? Ultimate answers to questions about the spiritual nature and meaning of life can come from only one source—the Intelligence that initiated it all. However one perceives or conceives a Creator God, that should be accepted as the original Source to start with without being locked into it.

If one or both parents have an interest in this topic for personal advancement, then consider introducing it to your children also after or while instructing them in what you determine to be a suitable belief system. Depending on their age and level of understanding, gauge their reaction and take it from there. Allow them a chance for an early start on their own personal quest.

Motivation and Open-mindedness

What does a seeker really want and why? The core motivation should be a sincere desire and drive to pursue knowledge of the nature and meaning of life—to understand the reason and purpose to exist. It should not be assumed that Illumination can progress directly from one's current beliefs and outlook of life if they are rigidly held. This would in effect be seeking, or expecting, confirmation of one's current beliefs, which would be a one-sided quest and therefore have limited scope. Likewise, seeking knowledge just for the sake of knowing or to satisfy a nagging curiosity is not good enough. Motive in this context is more than just having a desire for something—it must be a part of oneself, having a constant, fervent yearning to learn the origin and meaning of life. This goes hand in hand with being open-minded and tolerant of multiple belief systems.

It is not necessary to abandon one's current belief system in a quest for Illumination. A seeker should retain beliefs that encourage an intimate understanding of the Creator for as long as they are satisfactory to oneself, but they should not be treated as a boundary for inner development. Insight will come in forms or ways that are recognizable and will change only as the inner self develops. A person can be devout in one's current beliefs, but still be open to change if it comes from the Source, which can come only through personal experience. At some point, one question should be asked of oneself for contemplation, "Why do I believe what I believe?" How that is answered affects the progress along the path toward Illumination.

In the personal effort to gain knowledge direct from the G.I., being open-minded is all-important—being willing to reassess and revise opinions and beliefs incrementally when deemed sensible to oneself, not necessarily through convincing argument by others, but through insight gained from personal experience. Higher enlightenment and Illumination can bring knowledge that may differ from one's current beliefs and a seeker should be open to receive it. One can have ideas of what to anticipate if or when Illumination comes, but should not have expectations, which can be self-defeating. Expecting an experience to be a certain way limits what can be experienced and may even hinder what is desired. Knowledge and insight may come incrementally in small or large measure and in surprising ways at any time. Be aware that if or when answers come they may or may not agree with what is presently understood, but their validity will be felt. It helps to see one's current beliefs as being tentative, unless or until new insight brings a view that is more satisfactory to oneself. A balance between open-mindedness and skepticism is key.

Seek Answers from the Source

Contemplate often questions pertaining to the mysteries of life. Questions such as: What is the nature of a Creator God? What is the nature, purpose and meaning of life and how did it originate? Who and what am I really? What happens to personal identity after physical death? How can there be conscious, personal, realized contact with the Intelligence that is believed to be the source of all that exists?

The above sample questions and others about the mysteries of life should be pondered daily whenever possible so as to make it routine with little mental effort. What is needed here is frequency, not formality. Whether at work, recreation or leisure, make a concerted effort to remember to bring these questions and ponderings to the fore of the mind at least briefly throughout each day when it will not create a distraction or hazard to oneself or to others. This may be for a few minutes or as little as a few seconds at a time. Repetition is important. The object is to embed the yearning for answers within the subconscious mind so that it will be *felt* all the time without having to consciously think about it—like having it in the background without being distracting for daily activities.

This practice should become part of one's frame of mind for daily living (not just a procedure to follow) and a personal quest for answers from the Source— the Source being one's personal concept of the Creator God (what I choose to call the Greater Intelligence). Along with personal pondering it is easy to make the yearning for answers into a request directed toward the G.I.

It is of the utmost importance to be patient and persevere. Striving for inner development and answers to great questions should be a lifelong commitment regardless of the pace of progress. There may be long periods of time with no obvious moments of insight, but don't give up. Expecting recognizable results within any given timeframe will doom the effort. Insight comes when one is inwardly ready—and who or what determines when a person is ready? The G.I., of course, and it depends on one's sincerity and state of spiritual development in the present life.

There is no time schedule for progressing toward Illumination. Appropriate thinking can quicken advancement, but there should be no expectations. Time is a major factor in personal inner development and impatience is a killer. Having doubts about what one is doing or studying (as though on a trial basis) is self-defeating, but being simply uncertain allows greater possibility of receiving insight and is more conducive to learning. Intellectual openness is, of course, the first step, but enthusiasm can wane if no progress is perceived within oneself. There must be a genuine, committed motivation to ponder the nature and meaning of life regardless of all else.

As previously stated, prayer is more than speaking or thinking some words. It is the conscious direction of thoughts toward the G.I.—communicating and communing with the G.I. at any time, for any duration and it does not have to be formal or even linguistic. I recommend an informal, non-linguistic form of prayer that can be practiced anytime and anyplace. Language is a means for sharing thoughts among ourselves and though it serves us well, it is only a tool. Words, whether written or verbal, are simply symbols that represent thoughts. It is basically a way to translate thoughts, but no translation is needed for the G.I. When we pray what gets through to the G.I. are our thoughts, desires and feelings, which can be incompletely described and even muddled by words. Prayer in this manner is more like communing than communicating.

Words are necessary for a group prayer, but personal prayer can be without them. Initially it might be difficult to pray without their use so try to become acutely aware of thoughts and feelings before they would be expressed in words. Mental images can be used along with emotions, but few or no words. If there is a particular prayer or format that is favored, then concentrate on the meaning and feeling so that the words will no longer be necessary. When wanting to pray, resist the temptation to use words as much as possible until it becomes habit. Also, do not think of the G.I. as being somewhere "out there", but close at hand (in fact, within).

Without formality and words, one can pray almost anytime, anyplace, without being a distraction for other activities. Such praying can be very brief, but repeated often. Use this technique for all prayer, including the pondering of questions as stated above. When a group of thoughts and questions need to be pondered repeatedly, first convert them into a non-verbal yearning for answers and then associate a single word, symbol or image with those feelings. With success, thinking of that single reference should recall all the desires and sentiments in an instant.

This pondering and contemplation method of regular repetition when on the go is essentially equivalent to a casual form of meditation because it conditions the subconscious mind and can be more concentrated when relaxed in a quiet environment. With or without active thinking, one must have a receptive attitude for any insight that might come.

Spirit and Body

See the body for what it is—an organic machine. As marvelous as the body is and as attached as one is to it, it is still only a tool for one's use. It provides mobility, dexterity and has senses to monitor the immediate environment as well as the condition of the body itself. The spirit-identity of oneself is so integrated with it that it has no central location. Try to think of oneself as a pilot and overseer of this organic machine composed of a closed community of many types of specialized cells dedicated to a form for personal use. It is a partnership of the multitudinous lives of cells with the higher evolved spirit of oneself, which is comparable to the relationship that all lifeforms have with the G.I. With this, though, keep in mind that the G.I. is present in all forms and all things, but is recognized and acknowledged in this way only at the higher evolved levels. At the local level of a single human form one's spirit-identity is in every cell, but only in a functionally intact body, meaning that although cells, organs, blood and limbs can be removed and kept alive for a while the spirit of oneself stays with the whole of the remainder until it ceases to function.

The integration of spirit with body is so thorough that when we look at our own bodies or in the mirror at oneself it is natural to think "This is me", which is true in the sense that it physically identifies the spirit in this present life. Actually, though, it is more correct to think "This is mine" in order to emphasize the distinction between spirit and body.

Awareness of one's consciousness throughout the body can be improved by concentrating thought on all the body parts. The object is to concentrate less on thought activity within the brain and more on other parts to shift the focus of awareness and center of attention. I began doing this myself almost immediately after Illumination with the body as a whole during all my activities throughout the day every day, then later that same year devoting greater concentration on the individual parts while in a relaxed state. I also later learned that this relaxed form is a common technique practiced by others in various ways and sequences of going around the body.

Before proceeding further, it might be wondered if this outlook of one's own body makes any tangible or real difference in life. I can say that my own fervent effort to make this outlook routine is what directly led to my second Illumination. For a newcomer to this the initial practice might be little more than the imagining of extended awareness, but that will change in time with sincere effort.

Here is a simple method that works very well to emphasize the perception and perspective of one's body as "This is mine" rather than "This is me" so as to improve the balance between a spiritual and physical mindset. Although spirit and body are integrated for the lifespan of the body, spirit is distinguished as being separate-yet-connected with no fixed location. Think of your consciousness as extending outside the body, surrounding it like an aura, perceiving it both from within and without while controlling it from the cockpit (or driver's seat) that is the brain of this marvelous machine. Instead of manipulating your body automatically *as* your Self, condition your thinking to accept the body as a vehicle and tool *for* your Self. Every motion that you make is comparable to the control that you have when operating manipulative machinery (albeit with more exacting control)—you make it do what you want it to within its limitations. Try to keep this thought of extended consciousness active in the background of your mind throughout your active hours day after day (much like that stated in the subsection *Seek Answers from the Source* above) so that eventually it will become your norm—not just thinking it, but feeling it.

In conjunction with this mental practice (to which this goes hand-in-hand) there should be an effort to control the wandering of background thoughts, which improves mental discipline as well. The mind is naturally active and tends to fill in "idle" time (when not engaged and concentrating on some task) with other thoughts. This can also occur when doing routine tasks that are easy, repetitive or boring, so stray or wandering thoughts may be interspersed with the necessary actions. In these situations it is easy to daydream or recall music to pass the time away when the mind is only partially engaged. When this happens drop the stray thoughts and replace them with what is advised in these two subsections. Keep doing this for however long it may take for the desired thoughts to become automatic in the background so that you can feel them besides thinking them. You will have success when you realize that you "feel" the spiritual connection and yearning for esoteric knowledge all the time with less effort being spent to control the wandering of background thoughts. Now, this does not mean to try to eliminate daydreaming or other mental pastimes—only to control when it is done so as not to default to it.

In contrast to the practice described above that pertains to the perception and use of the body this next exercise deals with invigorating the communities of cells that compose it. The basic principle of focusing and concentrating thought within the body can be practiced in any number of ways to suit personal preference so that what I describe here is only suggestive to start with. Fundamental to my own practice is for the spirit that is oneself to exude love and thoughts of well-being upon all the cells of the body in similar fashion to how the G.I. permeates all matter.

This is to be done in a physically relaxed condition, so whether choosing to sit or lie horizontal do so to be completely comfortable so as to minimize sensory activity. Although silence is best to minimize audible distractions, if there is unavoidable background noise then play a recording of soft instrumental music. This can also be done beforehand to set a soothing mood if desired. When situated, close the eyes to eliminate visual distractions. Inhale slowly and deeply to fill the lungs to capacity, then slowly exhale to empty the lungs completely. Repeat this 2 or 3 more times before resuming normal breathing.

A good place to start focusing consciousness is the blood. Fix your attention on it as it flows in pulses delivering nutrients and oxygen throughout the body. Become acutely aware of its movement through the highways and byways that are the circulatory system—not just thinking about it, but feeling it as you stimulate the blood by your consciousness within it. Do this while feeling and directing gratitude for and to the work that the blood cells do for every part of your body—you should actually be thanking the cells directly. More than thoughts in the brain, place the emotion of gratitude within the cells to intensify awareness of the symbiotic relationship that you, as a spirit-identity, have with them.

Several minutes spent "connecting" with your blood in this way will invigorate it as you take a more active interest in its functioning. When successful you will feel a slight warmth all over. Now transition your attention to the heart as the blood flows through it. Direct gratitude to it for the hard work that it does to the keep the body going. Make the heart the focal center of consciousness to invigorate it just as you did for the blood. Dwelling on this for a minute or so will be fine.

The reason I like to start with the blood is because it reaches and affects every part of the body and is how I begin almost every session before switching to concentrating on specific parts. Use this technique to eventually cover all body parts in multiple sessions in whatever sequence you wish: blood; bones; organs (first individually); muscles; fingers, whole hands and arms, likewise toes, feet and legs; torso; and head. The head and neck in particular deserve detailed attention moving through the facial skin and scalp, eyeballs, ears, nose and nasal canal, brain, mouth and tongue, vocal chords and throat, skull, etc. A session might include only a few small areas, or larger areas expanding to take in the whole body. To reemphasize, focus consciousness on all parts to 'massage' and invigorate the cells with an attitude of gratitude and well-being. Time spent on a session could be 10-15 minutes until feeling positive results regularly then reduced to 5-10 minutes. If desired, this can be conveniently practiced in bed before sleep, which has the added benefit of relaxing mentally and physically as a prelude to sleep. One frequent side effect if this is done under a blanket is that the body may come to feel uncomfortably warm. Although this may be a subjective sensation, it feels real nonetheless and is an indication of a successful connection.

If you feel that one organ or area is weak then concentrate there for a session. As you gradually come to feel improved results, then adjust your time accordingly. You might even come to feel satisfied after only 2-3 minutes for a quick session.

Time duration is meant to be suggestive and can be whatever one feels comfortable with—do not be thinking of the passing of minutes while doing this.

A Choice of Methods

Since there are branches of mystical thought that profess possible repeatability and sustained duration of experiences in higher consciousness, it is proper to consider if they actually differ from Cosmic Consciousness as dealt with here or if they are only defined and reported differently by degree. This matter is mostly of concern to seekers to determine what type of experience and method of practice can best be related to for their own personal investigation and use. I have made no in-depth study of other methods because I feel no need to for myself, but others may want to make comparisons. For this, the following points are what I consider to be significantly defining in experiencing Illumination (as compared to ordinary cognitive experiences), which validate and support those noted by Dr. Bucke. His points are listed in chapter 5, *Some Words about Bucke.*

- The experience is extremely brief, but leaves a permanent effect on the recipient. Because of this permanency, there is no need to repeat it. [This expands on Bucke's point of brevity.]
- It is entirely non-physical, non-vocal and non-imaged. There is no sense of time, place or dimension and no awareness of one's body. Consciousness is 'felt' to be merged with a higher Intelligence within totality.
- It occurs without warning. The only apparent immediate condition necessary is to be somewhat relaxed mentally and physically. [This expands on Bucke's point of suddenness.]
- Personal thought is limited to passive awareness with no control over the duration or what is learned.
- What is gained is a profound metaphysical perspective of existence with comprehension by experiencing the complete unity that lies behind and within the physical universe. The volume of what is learned is tremendous considering the extreme brevity of time.
- The first instance is immediately followed by a flood of positive, uplifting emotions.
- A successive instance (if it comes) expands on the first without repeating it.

At this point it should be reiterated that Dr. Bucke originated the term *Cosmic Consciousness* for what he experienced and how he defined it. Unfortunately it is often used generically in reference to other experiences of higher or expanded consciousness that have different defining points. Since Dr. Bucke originated the term, its usage should be restricted to his definitive points and others only if they are supportive.

Concerning the point of brevity and permanency in particular, this brings us back to the matter of properly identifying an experience. The effects of Illumination do not fade with time so there is no need for a repeat. And, as previously explained in the subsection *Cosmic Consciousness* of chapter 2, a repeat of the same thing would be pointless. This alone sets it apart from other experiences that are reported to have a potential sustained duration of time and can be repeated. I can say nothing about the state or states of consciousness attained through other methods or how long the effects last in one's life, but that there is a difference in duration and that it can vary with each instance implies that there may be additional differences compared to the Cosmic Consciousness that Dr. Bucke wrote about and I as well now.

For whatever method a seeker chooses to use it is important to balance the needs and desires of the two sides of life—the physical and spiritual. Overemphasizing either one detracts from the purpose and usefulness of the other.

There Are No Shortcuts

All paths leading to Illumination are long and slow-going. This is spirit evolution at work that can be only somewhat quickened by natural, sincere effort that is put into it. The seeker must be on solid footing the whole way, which strengthens inner character and ensures steady progress. Some individuals, though, want to get dramatic results faster and think it can be found in the alternate mental states produced by certain psychedelic drugs and hallucinogenic substances. Certain drugs are purported to produce a mental state that sometimes has similarities to the unity that is experienced in Illumination accompanied with euphoria, but the user retains awareness of physical surroundings so that sensory input is mixed with whatever comes up in the mind. Time and space are factors in this, which makes the "trip" mind oriented, whereas true Illumination is spirit oriented with no time or spacial references whatsoever. Although some seekers using such substances might be pleased with what they experience, anyone choosing to do this is not in a position to know what might be genuine and what has been unwittingly altered because it all seems very real; an *altered* consciousness does not equate to a genuine *higher* consciousness.

Chapter 4

Supplementary Topics

Common sense is about as common as marshmallow pie.
MRU

[The following five subtopics that are touched upon are selected for their relevance and pertinence to expanding perspectives.]

Time

Time is a consequence of motion, of action, which equates to change. Although objects may be static within a local environment (i.e., from a relatively small perspective), universally nothing is truly at rest—dynamism is the rule. On larger scales (or wider perspectives) every material thing is in motion. What we call time, or time passage, is simply the changing positions of all material things relative to each other. What is of concern here is not how we choose to measure time passage, but rather with defining and understanding the three phases of time (i.e., present, past and future) from a universal perspective, which in turn affects our thinking about time in a broad sense despite variations in measurements.

Dynamism is inherent in the universe and is what distinguishes and defines what we call the present, which is only a fleeting instant, but followed by another instant and another and so on to produce a progression (or flow) of instants. This fleeting, dynamic current universe-wide present instant is the only instant in which thinking and actions can take place. It is universally simultaneous because *Thought is* the universe—It's aspect of the G.I. is innate in and through all that exists. This might seem irrelevant to us in a practical sense since we have to deal with the variances discovered within spacetime as they relate to our local perspective on Earth, but the relevance and value is in understanding the fundamental time phases universally.

Although universal simultaneity is beyond our perspective as individuals [Illumination gives a brief 'feel' for it through the universal consciousness that is the G.I.] it is not difficult to contemplate. If it were possible to take a 3-dimensional snapshot of the universe it would present a record of all positions of objects and events for a single instant. Now consider a series of such universal snapshots at equal universal intervals. This would show the sequence and timing of all motion and events as they occur simultaneously and how localized perspectives compare to the whole—the rate of universal time passage does not change for the G.I. We can speak of the present in relative contexts of the current time of day or the present age in which we live, but only the current instant is dynamic and separates past from future.

In contrast to the dynamic present instant, the past is static, unalterable. It exists only as memory, which is an intangible, nonlocational, non-dimensional record of all motion and experience—all events that have ever transpired from the instant they occurred in the then present. This is the memory of *Thought*, which is total. Exactly as with our own memory (which is a part of universal memory), it is subject to recall for review and can be reimagined or fantasized virtually, but this is an action in the present and in no way affects the record. With access to universal memory being almost non-existent for us outside of our own present lives (although some individuals can purportedly access it and some can recall parts of previous lifetimes) we must supplement personal and collective experiences with the memories of our predecessors (i.e., historical records—written or otherwise) and are limited to theorize, deduce, and guess about other past events.

Memory is the base for all learning and improvement on all scales, from a single lifetime of a single lifeform to the all-encompassing time up to now of the G.I. universally. Although individuals have imperfect memory recollection the G.I. has no such limitation; It cannot forget past events or unlearn things by changing them. The all-encompassing experiences within totality progress only forward with no backtracking so that any and all changes are made in the present with consequences for the future.

What we call the future is yet to be expressed by the G.I. and experienced by lifeforms—the word represents only potentiality for present dynamics. Prediction of future events is a matter of probability and depends entirely on the scale and type. While motions of objects that have regular and consistent patterns (such as celestial bodies of stars, planets, etc.) can be projected quite accurately, this is a matter of observation and calculation, not true prediction. For events on Earth, however, that have variable patterns of motion and are often subject to the behavior and independent decision making of lifeforms (of humans in particular), forecasts, predictions and prophesies can be little more than opinions based on trends that may indeed come true if the conditions that would lead up to them are not altered. Potential consequences of present and past actions might be foreseen in general only. Visions and dreams of things to come (whether the source is external to oneself or perhaps representing subconscious thoughts) might seem real, but are only virtual renditions of possibilities.

Supplementary Topics

If any or all future events could be known in complete detail and be unalterable so as to come to pass, then it would be no different than the static past and that would mean there could be no dynamic present. These three phases of time are contiguous, but do not and cannot overlap on a universal scale regardless of how they are perceived from local perspectives.

I do not deem it necessary to debate the idea of time travel beyond a mere mention of its impossibility, which is implied and intimated in the statements above. Time passage is not a dimension, but we put a measuring scale to it to track events which can give the impression of a dimension. Although there is no true interaction of the present instant with past or future, the idea is used for some fanciful and entertaining stories.

Exploitation of the Earth

There is a phrase that "home is where the heart is" (where a person likes to be), which is relative and can be applied to any scale. Although commonly used to refer to one's domicile, it is also used for the community or region in which one chooses and prefers to reside, continuing on to one's home state and home country. Whether an abode is small or large, primitive or extravagant, the residents do what they can to make their shelter suit their utilitarian needs as well as their desires for comfort—and just as we take care of our personal living quarters, so we also as communities cooperate to protect and maintain our joint home areas. There is one all-encompassing home that is shared by all, thus necessitating the cooperation of all people for its care and consideration and that is our planet Earth.

Although dominant, humans are only one lifeform among a myriad of others that are equally entitled by their very existence to suitable and sufficient habitat for their natural home territory. Emphasis is placed on 'home' to encourage sentiment for Earth and all its cohabitants, instead of seeing it and them as only resources for human exploitation. Although needed for food and used for products, plants and animals should be respected for the spirits within them and not be slaughtered or destroyed as mere objects. Even without intent to harm other life there is enough disregard and risk-taking in human exploitive activities to both potentially and actually jeopardize them and their habitat anyway. Methods and practices to extract what is wanted from land and sea on huge scales can be very destructive and damaging and waste and byproducts are often disposed of for convenience without regard for pollutive consequences. There will always be short-sighted people who care only about present needs and conditions and their actions and desires need to be offset or counterbalanced by leadership with long-term planning in mind. Likewise, short-sighted leaders should not disregard warnings of potential negative consequences of their decisions. We should all, as individuals and nations, be expanding our views of 'home' to a global scale for the sake of our descendants, ourselves and other lifeforms.

In recent decades we have been seeing escalating changes in environments around the world and the rate is accelerating. Whether this began naturally or not, human activities certainly exacerbate it and it is our obligatory responsibility to unite worldwide in efforts to reduce our own impact. The effects of industrial exploitation on a global scale across generations of our burgeoning populations are worrisome. Furthermore, imperiling the populations and survivability of other species (many to the point of extinction)—especially when there is intentional disregard—is a blight in the collective spiritual advancement of Man.

As is well known, unchecked population growth leads to its own downfall. We cannot ethically allow a person to die if it is within our ability to save a life and we have extensive medical knowledge and skills to do that, so we naturally seek to cure or lessen the impact of illnesses and diseases, thus extending our lifespans. There is no fault for simply following our survival instinct, but we overcome most of the natural checks on our populations. The ripple effects and consequences of local overpopulation can be seen historically and in recent centuries has been building globally with all its inherent stresses on wildlife and the Earth as a whole to an irreversible breaking point. The only reasonable solution seems to be for all people worldwide to voluntarily limit the number of children that they have to small numbers, but how likely is that to happen? Not all the consequences can be foreseen, but one that is certain is that if we humans cannot reduce and balance our impact on Earth with the needs of all other life, then eventually nature will forcefully balance it for us to our own detriment. It is a dilemma which I cannot ponder with optimism.

Past-life Memories

For some people—perhaps many—the thought of dying and then at some future time returning to Earth in another body with no memory of the present life is abhorrent. This should not impede their efforts to seek answers to questions regarding the mysteries of life in the manner that I suggest, but at some point maintaining a closed-minded rejection of at least the possibility of reincarnating will become an unwitting hindrance. Having an open-mind for whatever may come through communion with God (i.e., one's own personal concept and understanding) is imperative.

Without personally being able to recall memories prior to this current life it is easy to reject, or at least be skeptical of, the concept of reincarnation. Actually, skeptics see this as a concept (as did I in my younger years) whereas individuals who *can* recall such memories accept them as valid evidence and personal proof. There is only one difference between these memories and those from one's present life—one's Self is in a different body. The senses and sentiments within those clips of prior-life memories are as genuine as any from the present life and are readily distinguished from the remembrance of dreams or imagined experiences.

Adults who experience this phenomenal remembrance might initially find it puzzling if uninformed about it, but it should not be confusing as it certainly would be for a youth. Some of those bygone memories can come to the fore of consciousness spontaneously without forethought, but in my own cases I can only guess what might have triggered them. There is also an assisted means of accessing them through a past-life regression session in which a trained person guides the subject/patient into a random past incarnation without controlling it. It is not entirely random, though, for the life that is recalled will likely have some relevance in one's present life,

Spiritual Retribution and Escapism

Justice and retribution are necessary aspects in any society to encourage and enforce acceptable behavior, typically through some form of discipline or punishment that is deemed appropriate or commensurate for a bad deed or crime. The same principle holds true on a larger scale that extends across incarnations, but with a different means of correcting behavior, which I choose to call spiritual retribution—similar to, but not quite identical with, the concept of karma.

Spirit-identities incarnate into conditions (familial and otherwise) that the G.I. deems appropriate for expressive needs and/or to teach necessary lessons, but each spirit retains complete freedom of choice to deal with those conditions. Furthermore, conditions can potentially change in small or large part by the decision making of other people for their own lives that (intentionally or not) either directly or indirectly affect others. General conditions that are intended for a particular spirit may well remain in place, but their extent and intensity are subject to alteration. [Within this context it should be emphasized that the G.I. is not like a godhead passing judgement on spirits, dispensing fates that can progress only one way. The G.I. is the greater aspect of *Thought* influencing, not controlling, It's expression through us.]

Deeds and misdeeds done in one incarnation have consequences in one or more successive incarnations, but should not be thought of as reward and punishment. We cannot know or hardly even guess what conditions an individual will be born into next, but one thing needs to be said about hardened criminals and individuals who we call wicked, evil or tyrannical. Whatever they may do and whatever may be done with them in the present (or whatever they did in their lifetimes if they are deceased) it is tempting to ponder what hardships they may have to endure in their next lives. For the pain, suffering and sorrow that they caused to others they may very well have to experience it themselves—but not necessarily. There is no punishment in the spiritual sense, only lessons to be learned that progressively refine the expression of *Thought*, which for us on Earth means learning to live in harmony with each other, among other things. It may just as well be that an egregious person in one life may be presented with opportunities (and the ill-behaved spirit-identity may even have the desire after departing from this life) to compensate by being benevolent in the next. When that is not the case, though, if a spirit-identity remains recalcitrant regarding the guiding influence of conscience (remember that this is the subtle influence of the G.I within us), then lessons will be repeated indefinitely to encourage progress toward civility.

If there are desires and aspirations that remain unfulfilled at the time of one's physical death and are of sufficient intensity they can carry over into the next incarnation, whenever that might be and regardless of what the conditions may be. As a side note, this is the primary reason for natural, innate interests and inclinations that show up in some children early in their lives. Likewise, individuals that have a natural talent, ability or aptitude for particular things derive them from experiences in one or more past lives.

Life on Earth is not a utopia and never will be due to the great variation within human nature ranging from vice to virtue. When considering the struggles and challenges of life (social difficulties and hardships; crime of all kinds from petty theft and vandalism to murder; wars; pain and suffering through injury and disease; plus all types of what we call natural disasters) it is not uncommon to think of a spiritual existence as being comparably carefree and therefore preferable. Having wishes, hopes or dreams of a paradisiacal spiritual existence (or at least a pleasant untroubled one) after physical death is a means of coping with the hardships and all sorts of difficulties that are inherent in human life on Earth. This is an understandable aspiration as a reward for living a "good" life and (for a person from this viewpoint) is far more appealing than the implications of reincarnation, i.e., of additional lifetimes for better or worse. What this amounts to, though, is escapism—a desire to escape from the struggles of physical life by not having to repeat it. However, any thoughts of reincarnation being a repetitious cycle of unending trials, hardships or perhaps servitude to a higher spiritual power come from the ego within the limits of self-consciousness.

Along this same line of thought, but from a different viewpoint, is the idea that spirits eventually evolve to an upper state of enlightenment that would transcend the need for a physical body as though that were the goal of spiritual evolution, of life as a whole. What this amounts to is an idea of escapism on a vastly larger scale. Spirit-identities originate with the animation of matter and serve no purpose if they cannot reincarnate. It is the will of *Thought* to manifest and express and we (as spirits, not just human forms) are integral agents for that with infinite possibilities.

Cosmic consciousness dispels all thoughts of an end goal and instills a welcoming attitude for future expressive opportunities anywhere in the universe.

Demystifying Mysticism

What thoughts come to mind when hearing the word *mysticism*? How well is it understood? Despite the similar spelling to mystery and mystify, mysticism and mystics should not be mysterious. Although there are numerous varying descriptions of what mysticism is, the following is what it means to me as a recipient.

At the most fundamental level mysticism is simply having a sincere desire to personally interact with the Intelligence that is responsible for originating life and all else that exists (in one word, totality)—the Source of all that is. When the purpose for this is to seek an understanding of the reason for and meaning of life, it essentially merges mysticism with ontology, thus becoming the means for a personal inquiry into the nature of existence. It is not so important exactly what a person believes about such an Intelligence because this is more like a frame of mind—a personal effort to find understanding for what cannot be proven by others beyond doubt. It is or becomes a perspective of the spiritual side of life that is open for expansion and does not become a fixed set of beliefs. Outwardly a mystic may appear to conform to some particular belief system, but inwardly he is open to concepts beyond its boundaries. To limit oneself to a particular theology is to be religious only, whereas to accept a theology as a base for personal spiritual growth without its theological confines is to be religiously mystically inclined. Education provided by others regarding spiritual matters are taken as ideas to ponder and contemplate, but require verification which can only come from personal experience. The desire is to supplant beliefs with personally confirmed knowledge from the G.I., although this will still appear to be beliefs in the minds of others.

Although often associated with occultism due to its often misunderstood nature, mysticism is both natural and practical. There are no rituals or set practices to perform unless one chooses to and no dogma or doctrines to accept. With an open format (or lack of one) there is freedom to apply this frame of mind to established belief systems or make it independent, because this is a universal approach to the Intelligence at the core of existence. Whatever one's beliefs and understanding of a Creator God or supreme intelligence may be, a mystical frame of mind will build on it. Some religions have or have had a branch of mysticism within their teachings or among their more devout followers. In any case, though, as an individual's consciousness evolves there may be a desire or urge to search beyond one's current beliefs. Such an urge might show itself as a feeling of slight emptiness; that something is missing; that there is more to the spiritual side of life than what one is currently aware of. Response to this is a matter of conscience—what feels right for oneself.

All this should not be interpreted as criticism of religion for mysticism is complimentary to it and is a continuation and furtherance of beliefs (any beliefs) to better understand the deity (or whatever one chooses to call it). Beliefs should be seen for what they are—ideas and concepts that are accepted as being true, but cannot be proven. As such, acceptance should be tentative until some type of personal proof is found or experienced. This approach, or attitude, applies to all aspects of life and fully dominates our so-called scientific method of developing theories based on available data and evidence that are subject to change when additional pertinent information is obtained. Beliefs and theories are essential for incremental learning and should not be confined to particular viewpoints that dissuade further inquiry.

Due to the totally personal nature of mysticism it is not so much a field for study, except to learn what other mystically inclined individuals and organizations think, practice and teach. It represents a frame of mind and attitude toward life that can develop naturally for oneself or with help from others. Guidance and advice are all that can be obtained from others, but how can sound advice be determined when there *is* no such thing as credentials in this area? How does one qualify to speak competently about the experience of Illumination? Obviously the person must have experienced it himself, but acceptance of that and his words is dependent on his integrity and credibility as perceived by others.

Techniques and practices that are suggested to assist in striving for insight might be readily accepted, but acceptance of statements purported to be genuine spiritual knowledge should be tentative, as already mentioned. In matters of spiritual knowledge, personal experience and interpretation (whether correct or not) nearly always trump what others say. This is due to differences in perspective, what is sensible to oneself and what can be related to.

So who can be called a mystic? I'm not sure that there is a single good, straight answer for that. The word can be used in a specific way to mean an individual who has experienced Illumination or in a general way for anyone who is devoutly inclined toward mysticism. Personally, I don't care to assign titles to myself and hesitate to refer to myself as a mystic in conversation, but freely state that I have been mystically inclined all my life. To distinguish the two uses I use *recipient* for a full mystic in the specific regard, but perhaps *mystic* should continue to be used for both, with clarification. This is only a thought.

Chapter 5

Some Words about Bucke

For those who might not yet be familiar with *Cosmic Consciousness* by Dr. Richard M. Bucke, it was published in 1901 near the end of his life and has since become a classic on this subject. As a psychiatrist and professional medical practitioner he analyzed his own experience of Illumination (which he chose to call Cosmic Consciousness) and sought and obtained statements from contemporary individuals who claimed to have had similar experiences. Although he wrote little describing the actual event in his own life, he wrote at length about the evolution of consciousness, presenting it as a hypothesis from his professional viewpoint. Bucke's hypothesis and my description given in chapter 2 differ in details, but the defining points of the experience itself are the same. One notable difference, though, is worth mentioning: he used the words 'illumination' and 'intellectual illumination' a number of times in his book, but to my knowledge wrote nothing about where it might come from, apparently implying that consciousness merely evolves toward it.

Among his more significant findings and determinations is a list of 11 points that he believed are common to having the experience. They are listed below in a somewhat shortened description using his letter labels. Anyone who thinks he might have experienced Illumination can use points *a-h* as a check (which I concur as all being valid), because they are pertinent only to the recipient. Point *i* is just the recipient's age range taken from his research. Points *j* and *k* are observations made by others that the recipient would not know about if not told.

a. Having a sudden sense [not sight] of being surrounded by a flame or rose colored cloud, or that the mind is filled with such a cloud.
b. Feeling intense emotions of ecstasy, joy, assurance and triumph. [He also used the word *salvation*, but clarified it as being outside of the usual religious context.]
c. An intellectual illumination that is impossible to describe sufficiently. Some things that are learned are that the cosmos is a living thing; that all life is eternal; that the universe is ordered so that everything works together for the good of all; and that this expanded concept of the WHOLE is greater than what could be conceived, imagined or speculated through ordinary self-consciousness. The person will learn more in a few moments than through

years of study and much that no study can teach.
d. A sense of immortality of the spirit that is more than conviction.
e. There is no fear of death.
f. Loss of a sense of sin.
g. The experience is instantaneous and brief.
h. The previous character of the person is important.
i. A person's age at the time of illumination is important.
j. A certain charm is added to the personality of the person.
k. Opinion: During and shortly after illumination, the person's appearance changes.

Regarding point *a*, this could be Bucke's way of describing a loss of awareness of physical surroundings. For point *f* he provides no clarification, but it should be noted that sin is linked to a concept of God that is quite different from the Intelligence that is experienced in Illumination. Points *j* and *k* are subjective and can be validated only by other individuals.

Ending Comments

All the text of this book is written as straightforward as I can possibly make it at this point in my life. It represents my best effort to present an introduction and stimulus for contemplation of an amazing experience in the evolution of every spirit by relating the interweaving of intelligence and life with matter in a manner that is not overly complex. All in all, whatever we humans as individuals choose to believe about our origin and nature does not mean that that is actually so in a specific sense. Our challenge is to continually seek knowledge of our nature beyond what is currently accepted—to strive for personal Illumination, which continues afterward too.

Life after Illumination is neither easier nor more difficult than before, but is much more satisfying. As years become decades and decades pass, the effects of that very brief experience never fade.

There is one question that I have contemplated much during the writing of this book: If I could have read this very book or one similar to it during my younger unenlightened years, would I have been open to it? I likely would have been both intrigued by and skeptical of parts of chapters 1 and 2, but would not have rejected it outright. Aside from the stated general common points that agree with Dr. Bucke's findings, it probably would have been just another person's perspective to be aware of; after all, it is a testament of only one person. Likewise, this is the best that I can hope for the reader—simply to become aware of a perspective that goes beyond the individual.

Acknowledgements

I want to state my gratitude to three individuals who assisted directly or indirectly with the final form of my manuscript. There is my nephew-in-law Fernando Rodriguez Santander whose curiosity and interest in this topic caused him to ask me many questions (similar to the ones that I pondered in my youth) through correspondence spanning a number of years and answering them allowed me to refine some of the language and style that I would be using. My thanks also go to longtime friends Nancy Graham and Gene Turner for proofreading my draft and providing feedback. Equally important was the understanding and support of my wife, Jenny, throughout my many hours of sitting at the computer pondering and typing the text.

Images for the front and back covers are by courtesy of NASA and were chosen to give the impression of infinite space and time with the front image somewhat resembling the loose shape of an eye. The front was taken by the Spitzer Space Telescope and the back by the Wide-field Infrared Survey Explorer (WISE).

About the Author

Knowing the context and source is important for any information. With only testimony for evidence the reader may be wondering, "Who is this author?" Therefore, some things that set the foundation and direction of my early life that led to this profound experience should be shared.

Born in Lafayette, Indiana, but having mostly grown up in California, Lafayette remained my home away from home for as long as my grandparents lived. I grew up in a religious family that emphasized love of God in all that we do, which complimented my innate inclinations. From an early age onward I was well aware and remained aware of the depth of my desire to seek knowledge and understanding of the spiritual side of life (the root nature of things, as I told myself beginning in my pre-teen years); this was the driving force and main concern among my private thoughts. As early as the age of 5 or 6, I began to question (to myself, not verbally to others) some of the beliefs and traditional stories that I was taught. At age 7 I wondered about and seriously pondered the nature of

God. By my late 8th year I was aware that there are multiple religions and each professing a different view of God and the role of Man on Earth. I thought that if people pray to varying concepts of God and at least some of those prayers are answered, then they cannot be all wrong, neither can any one of them be completely right, but at least partly right in some way. Seeing that there were no definite answers to my greater questions about life, I felt that the only place to learn what was genuinely true was from the source, i.e., the Intelligence that created it all…God. The existence of God, or a supreme intelligence, was never in doubt by me—only how we perceive that Intelligence. Late age 8 was actually one of the most significant periods of my life for three decisions that I made.

1. I determined that the answers to my great questions about life *must* come from God so I began to seek direct communication (or communion) with the Creator and was open to whatever form it might take; to whatever content might be gained from it; accepted that the nature of God might differ from what was taught to me; and knew that it might be a very long time before having such contact. I realized this might be a lifetime commitment waiting for answers that may or may not come and that meant keeping the desire to

communicate active in my feelings (as a part of my Self), not just as a thought in my mind. From that young age onward I remained true to this commitment.

2. Knowing that there are many human languages I realized that they are arbitrary creations, I determined that natural communication with God would be nonverbal—more like using emotions, feelings and imaged thoughts, which are common to everyone. These are the sources of our thoughts, which we then translate into a communicable language among ourselves. So from that point onward, my personal prayers to God (or the G.I. as I much later came to say) have contained few words. Furthermore, I felt no need for an intermediary or supporter in prayer as I had been taught.

3. I had been taught that the human soul (spirit as I prefer to say) is eternal, but has only one physical lifetime. For a spirit to have only one life and then be in a heaven or hell for the rest of eternity (as I was taught) seemed like a waste to me. This left me open to the possibility of multiple lives, even though I could not accept what little I had heard about reincarnation. Specifically, I had heard that a human spirit could reincarnate as human or in

any lesser nonhuman form, but that did not seem right to me.

Questions about spiritual matters that I sometimes asked in my youth were typically answered unsatisfactorily and was told at least once that I "shouldn't think that way". Such answers and responses simply taught me to keep certain thoughts to myself; accept what others taught me only tentatively until I might hopefully someday learn directly from the Source (God); say what I was expected to say at home and church, although with some silent reservations; and continue to pursue my personal quest for answers. Perhaps because my search was personal and spiritual, I was not so familiar with or interested in the specifics of other religions or philosophies—and mysticism and the experience of Illumination were unknown to me.

Among my thoughts and innate inclinations during my early teenage years was an acceptance of the concept of evolution (i.e., the principle of gradual development and refinement), which I extended from the physical to include spiritual evolution (although I did not see the connection between them until years later). I simply perceived this as the means and method of creation. Despite these thoughts and others that I kept to myself, religion remained an important aspect of my life through my early adult years, as per my "policy" of tentative acceptance.

In early 1978 I was struck with a sudden, strong desire to read non-fiction books, whereas prior to that year my reading had been sporadic after my school years and was primarily of science-fiction books. I was initially drawn to ancient mysteries, specifically the subject of ancient knowledge and technology that was subsequently lost as indicated by extant surviving structures, artifacts and texts. In hindsight, this served to stimulate and provoke thought regarding forgotten or uncommon knowledge as an apparent prelude to what would come the following year. But, the desire to read non-fiction continuously has stayed with me ever since.

When Illumination came to me (of course, I knew no name for it at that time) just after my 27th birthday in January 1979, it was a wonderful and marvelous surprise beyond my imagination. The knowledge and insight that it gave me was what I had yearned for. I knew that it came in answer to my prayers and which aspects of my life contributed to it. Questions that I had pondered for more than 19 years were then answered.

As a side note here, a description of the circumstances of the timing of my experience exemplify how it can come quite unexpectedly. I was working in a machine shop on a Saturday morning when the shop was less active with fewer people than on weekdays. My job was to run an automatic (numerically controlled) lathe, which, although requiring my frequent attention, allowed me to periodically sit for just a few minutes. During one of those occasions I sat on a stool with my back leaned against a cabinet to relax physically and mentally, while not thinking of anything in particular (meaning that my mind was passive and therefore receptive), when it hit me. That was the instant of revolutionary change! I had made no immediate preparation and my preceding thoughts (prior to sitting) had been only on my work.

Despite feeling the inherent truth in what I gained from the experience, I had to seek validation of the experience itself because it was unique in my knowledge. It felt valid to me and I saw no detrimental effects, but was it real or a very realistic imaginative trick of the mind?

At a time when there was no internet to make quick and easy searches for information or to automatically suggest alternate searches, my search for verification began at the public library with books of science (I knew nothing about metaphysics or mysticism then), but I soon saw that physical sciences don't help in this. I also looked into the religious tenets and theology that I grew up with, but determined that they recognize personal development only within their own theological boundaries. After two months and not knowing where else to go I made a brief prayer for help and instantly the name *Rosicrucian* entered my mind. [Although it is easy to be skeptical of this, it is in fact true.] Although having grown up in San Jose (being the international headquarters for the Rosicrucian Order, AMORC, at that time), I was ignorant of anything more than its well-known Egyptian Museum and planetarium. Upon joining the Order and receiving the initial member literature it struck a chord within me, confirming that that was where I should be. It was through the Order that I acquired my first knowledge of metaphysical terminology to replace my religious vocabulary, which was quite inadequate for what I had experienced. I also learned from them for the first time the meaning of mysticism and saw that my own way of thinking throughout my life had been fundamentally mystically oriented.

Before this, though, almost immediately in that January, I began to apply the newly acquired perspective of life into my daily life. Progress was gradual, but led to a second Illuminating experience in January 1980. Its impact was quite different and presented a personal challenge, but provided supplemental knowledge to the first instance which further broadened my appreciation of existence.

Sometime within the latter part of that first year I came across Dr. Bucke's book *Cosmic Consciousness*. This is significant because it showed me that there are indeed others who have experienced genuine Illumination. Each of the points that Bucke determined to be common to the experience were part of my own experience. Even some of his wording is nearly identical to what I had been saying prior to reading his book. I no longer felt alone.

The driving force in the first 27 years of my life had been to gain insight into the nature and meaning of life. The personal nature and method of the quest, though, meant that there was no need to dedicate my activities or career to it. Unless a person is extremely skeptical about Illumination my experience can serve as a sound testament to its reality simply because I had no preconceptions of what to anticipate—there could be no auto-suggestion; it was beyond anything I could imagine. Although this was unique in my knowledge of human history at that time, I could not believe that it was truly unique to me alone. This was also one of the checks on myself to validate its authenticity. My method and attainment of Illumination was independent of all others. I still sometimes wonder if my progress might have been faster if I had known more about the topic in my younger years, but then, my life would not be the independent example that it is. Even though my yearning for answers was satisfied without help from others, I think it is better to make this topic more commonly known. Although I had the advantage of an innate desire for ontological knowledge through personal experience and the perseverance to stay with it, other youth and adults might have the interest, but not pursue it for lack of guidance, or might need only an introduction to spark an interest.

Now, it might be easy for a reader to wonder why, since my Illuminating experience occurred in 1979, so many years passed before writing and publishing this small book. I actually tried to express in writing what I experienced, how I felt and some of what I learned from it right from the start as well as jotting notes through the years for eventual selective compilation when I might be better prepared to do so, suspecting that it would certainly be after having raised my family and possibly even later. By the time I felt ready to begin I had become dissatisfied with my earlier efforts at presentation (not with the content, of course) and decided to start fresh, but this was not unexpected. Not considering myself to be a good writer, neither a good speaker, I was constantly at odds with myself about how to present the simplicity of one-ness within the context of a complex physical reality that others might be able to relate to. In the process I also decided to limit it to core information with few sidelines. Furthermore, I have not been greatly concerned about time, being more concerned about making this my best possible effort.

www.ingramcontent.com/pod-product-compliance
Lightning Source LLC
Chambersburg PA
CBHW020011050426
42450CB00005B/422